Recruitment Analytics: A Case Study on Online Recruitment and Selection Process using Principles of Project Management and MicroSoft Project (MSP)

By
Dr. Amit Phillora.
Phd(Recruitment and Selection)

And
Group Captain(Retd). BS Phillora
(Dean, ESCI, Hyderabad)

Recruitment Analytics: A Case Study on Online Recruitment and Selection Process using Principles of Project Management and MicroSoft Project (MSP) tool ©2019 by Dr. Amit Phillora.

All rights reserved. No part of this book may be reproduced in any form or by any electronic or mechanical means including information storage and retrieval systems, without permission in writing from the author.

Dairy Number:

1775/2019-CO/L

Dr. Amit Phillora

Visit my website at www. amazon.com/author/dr.amitphillora

Aknowlegement :

1. This book delves into the extensive literature that has already developed by eminent academicians, practitioners and researchers. The authors acknowledge these people for their works and ideologies incorporated in this volume.

2. The authors acknowledge, along with the publishers, the following reviewers for their invaluable feedback without which this book would have not come out in its present shape:

    (a)   Dr. Ashish Sharma, Sr. Lecturer, University Institute of Management, RDVV, Jabalpur.

    (b)   Dr. Suresh Naidu, Business Economics, Osmania University.

    (c)   Dr. Aparna Chakrabarti, Head of Department, Library, Osmania University.

    (d)   Dr. Sheshpal Namdeo, Assistant Professor, Management, APS University Rewa.

    (e)   Shri. DD Sharma, Former Joint Director Social Welfare & Panchayat Raj, Government of Madhya Pradesh.

    (f)   Dr. Shrinivas, Former Regional Head UGC Hyderabad.

    (g)   Dr. Ratnakar, Director and owner of IMRF.

    (h)   Miss Prabhjot Kaur, Asst. Professor, Communication Development (Delhi University).

    (i)   Dr. Vandana, Asst. Professor, SNS College Shehdol

3. The author also acknowledges the team of Kindle Direct Publishing for helping me in publishing the book.

*This book is dedicated
to
my parents Group Captain BS Phillora
and Rashmi Phillora*

Recruitment Analytics: A Case Study on Online Recruitment and Selection Process using Principles of Project Management and MicroSoft Project (MSP) tool.

Abstract:

The study focuses on Advertising Management in creating Online Ads for recruiting employee for MNCs. Using Project Management as an efficient and effective tool for managing the hire process for best employees for the companies with optimized expenditure and Time Schedule.

The study involves recruitment analytics. The study is based on Case Study which involves recruiting 30 employees in 60 days for upcoming Sales for Christmas month of December 2018 in an e-commerce company. We have used Microsoft Project Management (MSP) 2010 tool for calculating the Critical Path (CPM) to know how fast we can complete the complete recruitment process. We had used Job Posting and Resume Data Base Access (RDA) of Monster.com to study the Online Recruitment Process (ORP).

Keywords: Advertising Management, Project Management, Online Ad, Recruitment Analytics, Critical Path Method (CPM), Recruitment Database Access (RDA), Job Postings, Online Recruitment process (ORP) and Monsters.com.

Introduction:

Advertisement Management is heavily focused on the analysis, planning, control and decision-making activities of this core institution. Advertisement Management is a field which is made up of systems which interacts with organizations and institutions and this plays an important role in the advertisement process.

In this process advertisers play an important role. Advertiser is the core institution of the field of the advertising management and expenditure of the advisor provide the basis for estimate size of the advertising industry.

Major institution involved in Advertisement Management

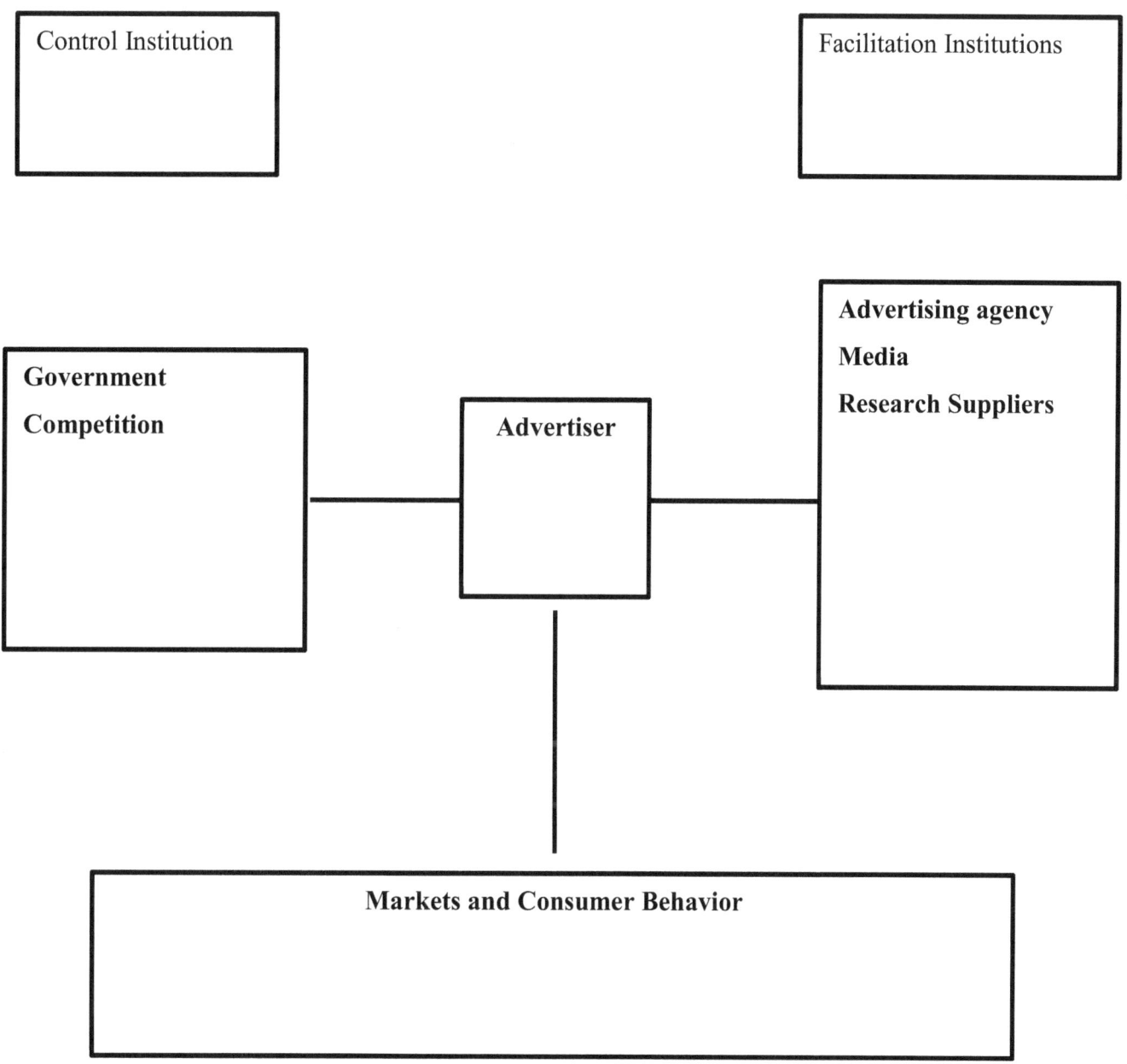

21st Century is the "Age of Internet". In the past, Print and TV were the only powerful media used for advertising. Now as internet being a powerful media, advertiser started utilizing Internet as medium for creation ads and promoters starts utilizing online advertising a powerful media.

Most Commonly used advertising or promoting media for free advertisements are as follows:

1. **Blogs**: Create Product Page and Market the products there and share it on different social media like Facebook, twitter etc.
2. **Create Facebook Page** where you can market yourself and show
3. **Companies**, Entrepreneurs create videos which explains about their companies their product lines. By this entrepreneur gets double benefits. If they cross the lower limits of the likes they get paid for the number of views and the visibility of their companies and product gets increased.
4. **Sponsor Ads** many companies post their ads in different websites by which the visibility of their companies and their products gets increased.

Concept of Project Management can play an important role in Recruitment and Selection Process and its analysis. We consider Recruitment and Selection as "Project" and it requires many activities to be completed.

Recruitment Process in an Organization

Case: Hiring 60 Customer-Care Permanent Employees for an e-Commerce Company for Dussehra and Diwali Peek. Number of days for hiring required are 60 days.

Approach to Solve the Problem:

We must study what is recruitment and Selection process and requirements for hiring employees in a company. The complete process is mainly divided into following 2 sub processes:

1) **Recruitment and Selection Process:**

   a) Job identification

   b) Vacancies needed

   c) Advertisement

   d) Test

   e) Selection of right candidates for the job

   f) Hiring and appointing

2) **Cost Analysis:**

   a) Budget estimation, analysis and approvals

Considering this Recruitment and Selection Process as a Project we will need to find out if we can complete the task in less than estimated 60 days and at a lower cost than estimated cost. Project Management will help us in optimizing the duration and the expenditure for the complete task without any compromise. This will be discussed in the subsequent paras.

According to Indian Calendar the Christmas is falling on December 25th, 2018. The new hires must get hired before at least 20 days before the festival season so that they can get trained and perform well during the festival season. Considering this we'll be following principles of project management using software Microsoft Project (MSP) 2007. Other versions of this software can be used or other softwares like primavera etc also can be used for optimizing the time duration and the cost. The software has the potential to develop plan of the complete process. One can use "what if analysis" to identify the uncertainties in the projects, identify the risk involved in the process and prepare possible plans to overcome that so that probability of success of the project can be ensured. Once the plan is frozen, the software during actual execution also helps in monitoring and exercise controls on the the process activities and cash flows.

Duration of the project can be initially found out by working out using pragmatic systematic and scientific approach. Exploring what if analyses using software the shortest possible project duration (Critical Path) can be identified. This will help the recruiters in tracking and completing the recruitment process well before the estimated time of completion.

Before we get into the details of solving the research problem let us know what project, project management and Network Analysis is.

a) **Project:** A project defines combination of inter related activities which must be executed in a certain order to complete the entire task. The activities cannot start until some others are completed. In this case recruiting 30 employees for an MNC in 30 days is a project.

b) **Project Management:** Project management is the practice of initiating, planning, executing, controlling, and closing the work of a team to achieve specific goals and meet specific success criteria at the specified time. ... The primary challenge of project management is to achieve all the project goals within the given constraints.

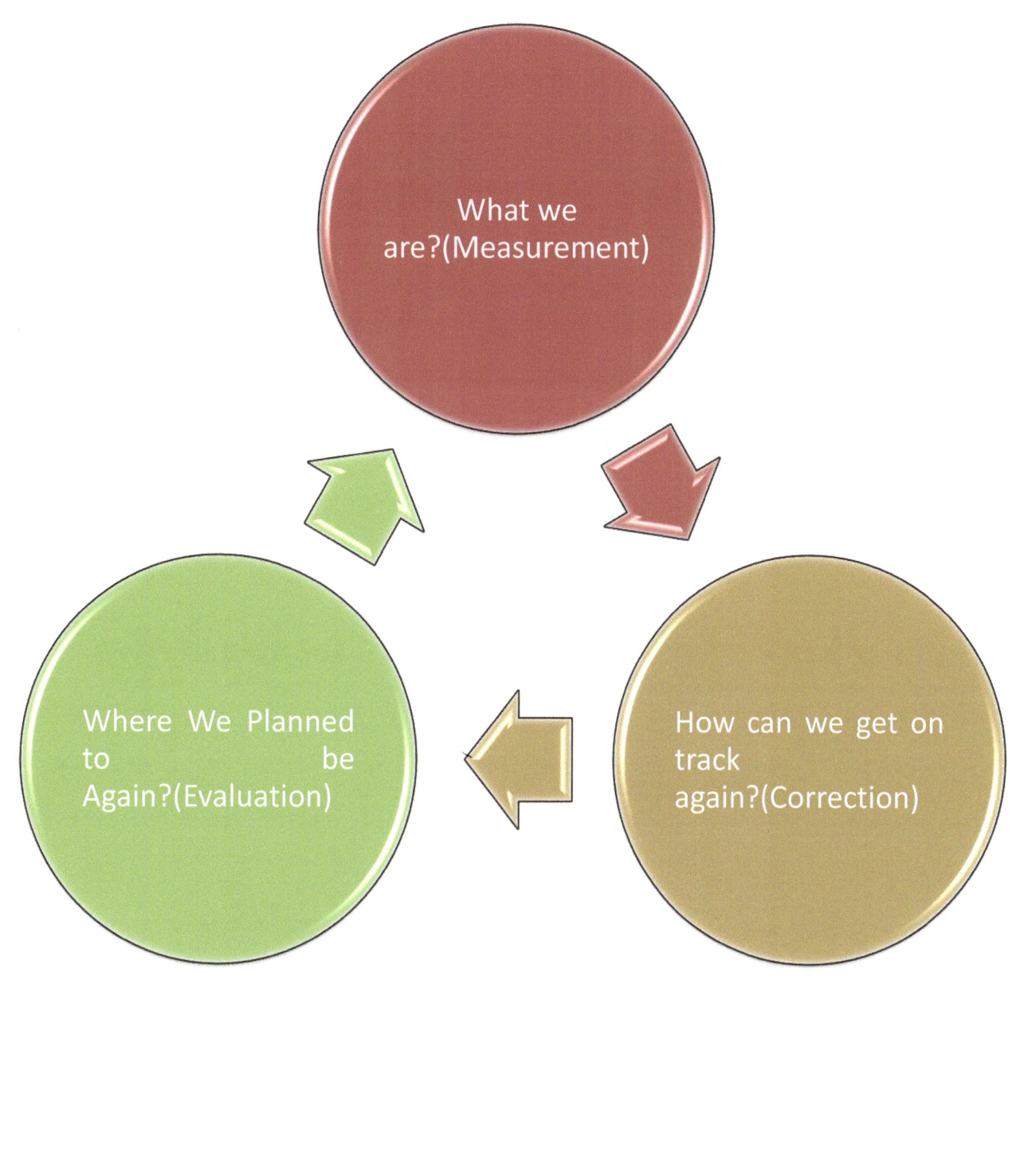

c) **Network Analysis:** Network analysis is the analysis of network, which is a graphic depiction of 'activities' and 'events', the planning, scheduling and control of a project.

What is Critical Path Method (CPM) in Project Management?

In project management, a critical path is the sequence of project network activities which add up to the longest overall duration, regardless if that longest duration has float or not. This determines the shortest time possible to complete the project. There can be 'total float' (unused time) within the critical path.

The sequence of critical activities in a network is known as Critical Path (CP) and it's the longest path which defines or gives the minimum time required to complete the project.

The length of the CP is the sum of individual times of the Critical Activities (CA) lying on it and defines the minimum time required to complete the project.

CA are those activities in a network the delay of which will cause further delay of which will cause further delay in the project completion time. All activities having zero total float value are identified as CA.

Recruitment Analysis done by using Project Management Software: MSP 2007

Utilization of concept of project management in recruitment and selection process

1. In the subject case the time for completing the Recruitment and Selection (R&S) process by a particular company was estimated to be 60 days.

2. The Budget for the expenditure was estimated to be Rs. X

3. Certainly Management wanted to optimize the entire process of Recruitment and Selection to have efficient and economical solution

4. In order to have this it was decided to use the concept of Project Management for completing the R&S process in as less time as possible and at as low expenditure as possible. For this, various Concepts of Project management was utilized. These are given below:

5. **Work Breakdown Structure**.

   (a) The Recruitment and selection process were broken in to various activities.

      (i) Considering this case as a project we found following are the activities to complete this project.

      (ii) Job Identification by a Department in an MNC;

      (iii) Consolidation of Job Vacancies for recruitment in an MNC;

      (iv) Financial Acceptance: Budget Analysis;

      (v) Preparation of job posting: Prepare the QR for the posts required to be filled;

      (vi) Mode of Advertisement;

      (vii) Online Job posting and Recruitment Database Access (RDA): Monster.com;

      (viii) Results for recruitment by RDA;

      (ix) Recruiting Staff contacting eligible candidates;

      (x) Inviting candidates for interview process:

         (aa) Aptitude test;

         (ab) Psychometric Tests;

         (ac) Interview;

      (xi) Selection Process:

         (aa) Offer letter to the Selected candidates;

    (ab) Contract and Legal document signature process;

  (xii) Acceptance and Appointment letter.

(b) Estimation for time duration: Initially it was assumed by the author.

(c) Relationship between the activities was identified. Initially the Finish to Start relationship was only assumed. The table prepared I given below;-

Table 1: List of activities Using WBS, Precedence relationships and estimated durations.

Activity SL No	Activity	Duration	Relationship	Precedence
Project Name	**Recruitment & Selection through online advertisement**			
1	Starts			
	Vacancies Identification			
2	Department in an organization Identifies the Vacancies	3	FS	1
3	Organization consolidates and Finalize the requirement of vacancy	3	FS	1
4	Job wise analysis and examination and finalization of the vacancies by HRD	2	FS	2 & 3
5	Financial Recommendation	3	FS	4 & 3
6	approval by the competent authority	4	FS	5
7	HRD prepares the QR for the posts required to be filled	5	FS	6
8	Advertisement for Filling Vacancies		FS	6
9	HRD study Mode of Advertisement	1	FS	8
10	HR department identifies and selects on line using Job portals	3	FS	9
11	Registration with job portal	3	FS	10
12	Job Portal provided list and contact detail of The Eligible candidates	3	FS	11
13	Personnel Department contacts eligible candidates and Sends Call letters	5	FS	12
14	On Line Test	1	FS	13
15	Written Test	2	FS	14
16	Interview	3	FS	15
17	selection		FS	16
18	offer letter	3	FS	17
19	contract and legal document signature (company policies	1	FS	18
20	Acceptance/Appointment Letter	3	FS	19

6. **Network Diagram** A network Diagram was prepared and used as a basic planning and discussion tool.

Fig1: Network Diagram By drawing simple network the activity optimization reduced the duration from estimated 60 day to 48 days.

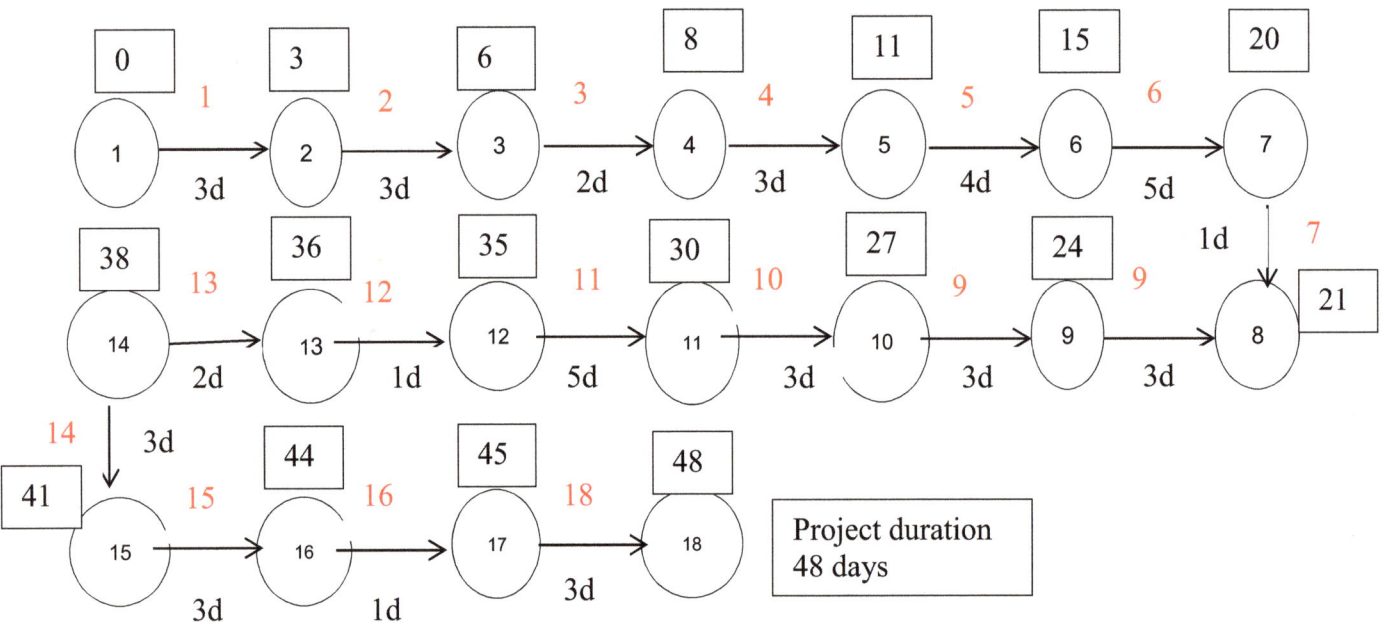

7. Analysis of the network was done to find out following important information

   (a) Identification of Critical Activities

   (b) Based on the Critical activities calculating the project Duration.

8. Network diagram was discussed with each activity/ process owners in a brain storming process for optimizing R&S process in following:-

   (a) Finalize the activities sequence

   (b) Realistic time estimation for completing each activity.

   (c) Realistic cost estimation for completing each activity

   (d) Discussion on each activity and its relationship with the previous and later activities.

   (e) Feasibility of doing some activities concurrently.

   (f) Resources both manpower and, material needed to do the activity.

(g) Finding out budget for conducting each activity.

(h) Based on these input finding out project duration and project cost.

9. Optimization of R&S Process. All relevant data was fed in the MSP 2007 Software. And it was utilized for finding out Project Duration Budget and cash flow.

10. **Step-1:**

(a) Using the "What if analysis" a special feature of MSP 2007, further optimization was achieved.

(b) Using concept of work breakdown structure, Rough estimation of the budget and duration of selection and recruitment the entire activities were listed down. Initially finish to start relationship among all the activities was assumed. That means one activity is to be done after the completion of this first activity.

(c) Based on this concept the project management duration was worked out to be 60 days

11. **Step-2:**

(a) Subsequently the individual activities was studied and the individual department concerned were discussed as to,

   (i) In which all the activities they can cut down the time and cost, to refine the estimates earlier taken.

(b) With this process of reassessment and examination of the actual activities with the activity owners it was found that the project duration from 60 days does come down to 48 days

12. **Step 3**

(a) Subsequently the brain storming with process owners was done to find out which activities can be done concurrently. For example Activity Sl No 4: Department in an organization Identifies the Vacancies and Activity Sl No 5 : Organization consolidates the requirement of vacancy can be done concurrently.

(b) It was found that four such activities could be identified which can enjoy the relationship of start to start

(c) with this the project duration finally got reduced to 36 days

13. **Benefits of using the PM Concept**

(a) Thus it can be seen that PM Concept provides systematic us step by Step by systematic Solution to optimize the R&S Process.

(b) The procedure developed if explored further can further provide further reduction of cost and time duration, by fine tuning each Activity by optimizing the work content

(c) The data fed on MSP 2007 is also available for further analysis and optimizing the process by conduction What if Analysis many uncertainties can be resolved, midterm correction can be incorporated and real time monitoring & Control can be exercised.

(d) The Procedure & System Developed can also be used as a tool for imparting training to the people involved in entire Process of R&S.

(e) This give innovative and creative idea to delete redundant steps taken or add the realistic step with relativistic Time & Cost estimates.

(f) User can conceive idea related to required infrastructure and support

(g) Software help us in generating various report for top management on the status of the process at desired intervals, both the physical performance as well as the financial performance can be checked with proper monitoring and control during the entire process

(h) It can also help us in generating the cash flows for advertisement and entire process. It helps in acquiring the required cash or amount to meet day to day or weekly expenditure.

(i) The steps mentioned above also produces a checklist for the entire process and leave no chances for any mistakes due to omission, by individual.

Research Problem: To recruit 60 employees in an e-commerce Multi-National -Company (MNC) in 60 Days for upcoming Christmas Sales in December 2019.

Research Tool: Microsoft Project Management (MSP) 2007.

Research Method: Calculation Critical Method (CPM) using MSP tool.

Sequence of Activities

Original

Project Duration 41 days

Precedence relationship: FS

First Optimsation:

Optimization using MSP 2007 and Project management concept
Concurrent activities:

SL No	Activity	Duration	Relationship	Precedence
	Selection through online advertisement			
1	Starts			
	Vacancies Identification			
2	Department in an organization Identifies the Vacancies	2.5	FS	1
3	Organization consolidates and Finalize the requirement of vacancy	2.5	SS	1
4	Job wise analysis and examination and finalization of the vacancies by HRD	2	FS	2 &3
5	Financial Recommendation	3	FS	4&3
6	approval by the competent authority	4	FS	5
7	HRD prepares the QR for the posts required to be filled	5	FS	6
8	Advertisement for Filling Vacancies		FS	6
9	HRD study Mode of Advertisement	1	SS	8
10	HR department identifies and selects on line using Job portals	3	FS	9
11	Registration with job portal	3	FS	10
12	Job Portal provided list and contact detail of The Eligible candidates	3	SS	11
13	Personnel Department contacts eligible candidates and Sends Call letters	5	FS	12
14	On Line Test	1	SS	13
15	Written Test	2	FS	14
16	Interview	3	FS	15
17	selection		FS	16
18	offer letter	3	FS	17
19	contract and legal document signature (company policies	1	FS	18
20	Acceptance/Appointment Letter	3	FS	19

Rational Estimation of Individual Activity Duration

Precedence Relationship optimization

Project Duration 38 days

ID	Task Name	Duration	Start	Finish	Predecessors	Resource Names
1	Selection through online advertisement	38 days	29 Sep	21 Nov		
2	Vacancies Identification	17 days	29 Sep	23 Oct		
3	Starts	0 days	29 Sep	29 Sep		
4	Department in an organisation Identifies the Vacancies	3 days	01 Oct	03 Oct	3	Department Head,Staff
5	Organisation consolidates the requirement of vacancy	3 days	01 Oct	03 Oct	3SS	Department Head,Staff
6	Job wise analysis and examination and finalisation of the vacancies by HRD	2 days	04 Oct	05 Oct	5,4	Department Head,Staff[10]
7	Financial Recommendation	3 days	08 Oct	10 Oct	6,5	Department Head,Staff[5]
8	approval by the competent authority	4 days	11 Oct	16 Oct	7	Operations Head,Staff[4]
9	prepare the QR for the posts required to be filled	5 days	17 Oct	23 Oct	8	Content Developers[3]
10	Advertisement for Filling Vacancies	12 days	24 Oct	08 Nov	9	
11	Mode of Advertisement identified	1 day	24 Oct	24 Oct	8SS	Staff,On Line Portal Expenditure[2]
12	HR department identifies and selects on line using Job portals	3 days	25 Oct	29 Oct	11	Department Head,Staff[4]
13	Registration with job protal	3 days	30 Oct	01 Nov	12	Staff
14	Job Portal provided list and contact detail of The Eligible candidates	3 days	02 Nov	06 Nov	13	Tele recruiters[5]
15	Personnel Department contacts eligible candiadtes and Sends Call letrs	2 days	07 Nov	08 Nov	14	Recruitment Team[3]
16	Test	4 days	07 Nov	12 Nov		
17	On Line Test	1 day	07 Nov	07 Nov	15SS	
18	Written Test	2 days	08 Nov	09 Nov	17	Department Head,Staff[9]
19	Interview	3 days	08 Nov	12 Nov	18SS	Department Head[4],Operations Head[1.33],Staff[6.67]
20	selection	7 days	13 Nov	21 Nov		
21	offer letter	3 days	13 Nov	15 Nov	19	Staff[2],Department Head
22	contract and legal document signature (company policies)	1 day	16 Nov	16 Nov	21	Staff,Department Head
23	Acceptance /Appointment Letter	3 days	19 Nov	21 Nov	22	Staff
24	End	0 days	21 Nov	21 Nov	23	

Project Duration :36 days

SL No	Activity	Duration	Relationship	Precedence
	Selection through online advertisement	**36 days**		
1	Starts	**16 days**		
	Vacancies Identification	0		
2	Department in an organization Identifies the Vacancies	3	FS	
3	Organization consolidates and Finalize the requirement of vacancy	3	SS	
4	Job wise analysis and examination and finalization of the vacancies by HRD	2	FS	
5	Financial Recommendation	3	FS	
6	approval by the competent authority	3	FS	
7	HRD prepares the QR for the posts required to be filled	5	FS	
8	**Advertisement for Filling Vacancies**	**9days**	FS	
9	HRD study Mode of Advertisement	1	SS	
10	HR department identifies and selects on line using Job portals	3	FS	
11	Registration with job portal	3	FS	
12	Job Portal provided list and contact detail of The Eligible candidates	3	SS	
13	Personnel Department contacts eligible candidates and Sends Call letters	2	FS	
14	**Test**	**4 days**	SS	
15	On Line Test	1	FS	
16	Written Test	2	FS	
17	Interview	3	FS	
18	**Selection**	**7 days**	FS	
19	Offer letter	3	FS	
20	contract and legal document signature (company policies	1	FS	
21	Acceptance/Appointment Letter	3	FS	
22	End	**0 days**		

Output from MSP 2007

ID	Task Name	Duration	Start	Finish	Predecessors	Resource Names
1	**Selection through online advertisement**	36 days	29 Sep	19 Nov		
2	**Vacancies Identification**	15 days	29 Sep	19 Oct		
3	Starts	0 days	29 Sep	29 Sep		
4	Department in an organisation Identifies the Vacanci	2 days	01 Oct	02 Oct	3	Department Head,Staff
5	Organisation consolodates the requirement of vaca	2 days	01 Oct	02 Oct	3SS	Department Head,Staff
6	Job wise analysis and examination and finalisation of the vacancies by HRD	2 days	03 Oct	04 Oct	5,4	Department Head,Staff[10]
7	Financial Recommendation	3 days	05 Oct	09 Oct	6,5	Department Head,Staff[5]
8	approval by the competent authority	3 days	10 Oct	12 Oct	7	Operations Head,Staff[4]
9	prepare the QR for the posts required to be filled	5 days	15 Oct	19 Oct	8	Content Developers[3]
10	**Advertisement for Filling Vacancies**	12 days	22 Oct	06 Nov	9	
11	Mode of Advertisement identfied	1 day	22 Oct	22 Oct	8SS	Staff,On Line Portal Expenditure[2]
12	HR department identifies and selects on line using Job portals	3 days	23 Oct	25 Oct	11	Department Head,Staff[4]
13	Registration with job protal	3 days	26 Oct	30 Oct	12	Staff
14	Job Portal provided list and contact detail of The Eligible candidates	3 days	31 Oct	02 Nov	13	Tele recruiters[5]
15	Personnel Department contacts eligible candiadtes and Sends Call lettrs	2 days	05 Nov	06 Nov	14	Recruitment Team[3]
16	**Test**	4 days	05 Nov	08 Nov		
17	On Line Test	1 day	05 Nov	05 Nov	15SS	
18	Written Test	2 days	06 Nov	07 Nov	17	Department Head,Staff[9]
19	Interview	3 days	06 Nov	08 Nov	18SS	Department Head[4],Operations Head[1.33],Staff[6.67]
20	**selection**	7 days	09 Nov	19 Nov		
21	offer letter	3 days	09 Nov	13 Nov	19	Staff[2],Department Head
22	contract and legal document signature (company policies)	1 day	14 Nov	14 Nov	21	Staff,Department Head
23	Acceptance /Appointment Letter	3 days	15 Nov	19 Nov	22	Staff
24	End	0 days	19 Nov	19 Nov	23	

Findings:

1. The project will get complited in 47 days if done with normal pace.

2. By using project management we could find some parrell activities and could finish the entire project in just 36 days.

3. This will help the training team in having more number of days for training the employees for upcoming peak.

Result : CPM for the Project is 36 days

Biblography:

1. Karminder Singh Ghumman & K Ashwathappa, 2010, Management :Concepts, Practice & Cases, New Delhi , MC Graw Hills . ISBN-10:0-07068218-4.

2. Rajiv Batra,1996,Advertsing Management, ISBN-10:81-7758-850-8.

3. K Ashwathappa, 2005,Human Resource and Personnel Management, ISBN-10:0-07-059930-0

4. Quatittative Techneques For Descision Making , Sure Publication, edition 2007.